I0539993

Psychological Development of Man as Expressed Through Biblical Themes

Psychological Development of Man as Expressed Through Biblical Themes

BONNIE L . NOREM

ARPress
ILLUMINATING IDEAS
EMPOWERING VOICES

All biblical references are to the Jerusalem Bible.

FIRST EDITION

Copyright © 2025 by Bonnie L. Norem.

All rights reserved. No part of this publication may be reproduced, distributed, or transmitted in any form or by any means, including photocopying, recording, or other electronic or mechanical methods, without the prior written permission of the copyright owner and the publisher, except in the case of brief quotations embodied in critical reviews and certain other noncommercial uses permitted by copyright law. For permission requests, write to the publisher, addressed "Attention: Permissions Coordinator," at the address below.

ARPress
45 Dan Road Suite 5
Canton MA 02021

Hotline: 1(888) 821-0229
Fax: 1(508) 545-7580

Ordering Information:
Quantity sales. Special discounts are available on quantity purchases by corporations, associations, and others. For details, contact the publisher at the address above.

Printed in the United States of America.

ISBN-13: Softcover   979-8-89676-253-9
          Hard   979-8-89676-257-7
          eBook   979-8-89676-254-6

Library of Congress Control Number: 2025904630

Table of Contents

Preface vii

Introduction ix

PART I: Individual Stages In Man's Development 1

    1. Disharmony 3
    2. Foreign Land 5
    3. The Call 9
    4. A Covenant 14
    5. Wilderness Experience 16

Part II: Call to Wholeness 21

    6. Running Away 25
    7. Storm of Life 27
    8. Depths of Suffering 30
    9. Rebirth 32

Part III: Community Development 37

    10. Faith 41
    11. Forgiveness 44
    12. Treatment of Forgiving 50
    13. Rituals 57
    14. Discipline 62
    15. Healing 65

References 69

Bibliography 71

Preface

This paper was written as a thesis while I was at George Mason University. My interest in psychology began back in the '60s and then really blossomed in the '70s. In June 1972, our family was caught in the Agnes flood and there was water ten feet high on the outside of our house. Our basement was completely filled with water, with ten inches of water on the first floor. Most of our library was in the basement, and when we were cleaning up after the flood, there were two books caught in the rafters of the basement ceiling. They were completely dry, whereas everything else in the basement was completely destroyed. Those two books were Viktor Frankl's book, *Man's Search for Meaning*, and Carl Jung's book, *Modern Man in Search of a Soul*.

Rereading these two books after the flood helped give me new hope and meaning. I became interested in man's quest for life and in 1976 decided to return to college once again and study psychology. I was very disappointed to find that academics still did not consider the spiritual side of man and some did not even emphasize the physical. In 1971 I started to take my dreams seriously and have found through the years that this is one way God does speak to man today to help direct our lives. God is still active and alive in forming our lives and directing us to become the people we are to become.

Introduction

Many psychological readings today deal with the seasons of man's life. These seasons may be called transitions or stages of life.

Daniel J. Levinson's book, *The Seasons of Man's Life*, deals with stages of man's adult life. Man in his early twenties deals with the polarity of dream/reality. In his thirties he should be settling down/moving on. Man then finds his niche/climbs the mountain, is/ becomes. A later stage deals with the polarities of man as he is/could be. Finally, man must deal with the mortal/eternal.

Gail Sheehy's *Passages* took off on Levinson's theme and dealt with the transitions of life. She talks about a transition or career reassessment occurring around thirty. She saw again a midlife crisis occurring between thirty-eight and forty-five, when people reassess their goals and then reestablish their lives.

In looking at the stages of man's life, we need to see them through history. We have many different sides, and only by looking back can we look forward with power and affect. It is in looking back and learning from the past, a past that can't be changed, that we can utilize it in molding our lives today.

The Bible is one rich source for dealing with the seasons of life. This book will express some transitions and sources of conflict as found in the Bible in relationship to individual and community development. It also will express a means for growth of unity. The Bible is a history of man's walk in life in relationship to God. This relationship may be seen as a unity developing within man's life.

Each person does have an *ultimate concern* for life. This book will look at this concern as a religion. Rollo May (1933) states that religion is based on the assumption that life has meaning. Religion, or the lack of it, is not shown in some intellectual or verbal formulation, but we see it in one's total orientation to life.

The biblical events help focus more clearly the *spiritual existence* in which man is made more humanly alive. This spiritual existence implies responsibility and the bringing of the self to consciousness. Frankl (1965) saw that only the religious person is able to bring religion into psychotherapy. Irreligious psychotherapy never has the right to manipulate the patient's religious feeling by employing religion as a tool, such as a pill or shock treatment. Religion provides man with more than psychotherapy ever could, but it also demands more of him!

John Drescher (1979) told a story about a British schoolmaster who was asked where in his curriculum he taught religion. He said:

We teach it all day long. We teach it in arithmetic by accuracy . . . in language by learning to say what we mean . . . in history by humanity . . . geography by breadth of mind . . . in handicraft by thoroughness . . . in astronomy by reverence . . . in the playground by fair play. We teach it by kindness to animals, by courtesy to servants, by good manners to one another, and by truthfulness in all things.

This story illustrates how our religion is our meaning for life.

These concerns or religious attitudes can be destructive as well as constructive. *Psychology Today* magazine (1976) described an example of a destructive attitude. An experiment in Nazism was conducted on a high school class. Students initially could not imagine how the Germans could become caught in such a movement. The teacher started using the key Nazi concept of discipline to control the class. Students were encouraged to leave the experiment at any time. The students became caught up in the movement and accepted the discipline without question. Amazingly, within five days the class grew from thirty students to two hundred. They went along with the movement believing there was a Third Wave taking over.

Adolescence is a time one starts developing *identity*. The development process is often expressed as a whole person supported by a tripod made up of the physical, mental, and spiritual (moral) developments. These overlap and affect each other. We cannot divide a person into three equal parts—body, mind, and spirit—but we need to look at the whole person as made up of all three. In the interrelationship, one part may stand out more than another part, but they will all affect each other and be interlocked (as illustrated by the following diagram).

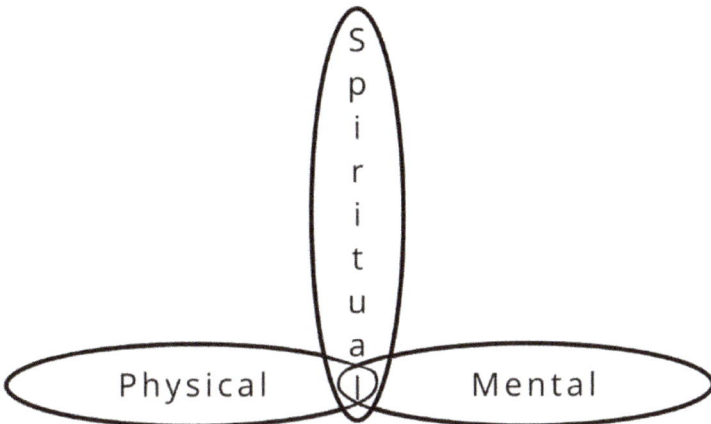

Our individual makeup may help govern this. As the figure shows, one may be physically strong and not excel in the other two areas. This may be due to a social setting that stresses physical ability or it may be inherited.

Each of these three strengths affect each other and can help one to be more creative when they are in tune with each other psychologically. It is strange that in our society we have veered away from the spiritual tripod. We can see this as part of our tearing away the onion peel to get to the inner core. When we divide these areas and do not allow one to develop, we repress part of ourselves, resulting in an *identity diffusion*.

Psychological Development of Man As Expressed through Biblical Themes

PART I

INDIVIDUAL STAGES IN MAN'S DEVELOPMENT

1. DISHARMONY

The Bible starts with man falling out of harmony with self, God, and others. This is seen in the story of Adam and Eve. Scripture says man's inner conflicts and dilemmas come to us through *disharmony* with God, a falling away from God. This is described as *sin*. Sin is defined as a breaking away from God and the rest of humanity, a partial alienation or act of rebellion. Sin is missing the mark.

Karl Menninger (1974) noted that analysts do not use the word *sin* but refer to aggressiveness and self-destructive behaviors. These bring with them the implication of guilt, reparation and atonement. The analyst cannot decide what is sinful for his patient, but he can say that aggressiveness and self-destructiveness are evil.

Menninger said calling something a *sin* and dealing with it as such may be a useful salvaging or coping device. When there is something within a person that is seen as destroying him, it should be pointed out. If the person has symptoms stemming from a sin, those need to be dealt with. For example, when a person has cancer, the person is told the basis of his problem, and the symptoms from the cancer are dealt with. It does little good to repent a symptom, but it may do great harm not to repent a sin. Vice versa, it does little good merely to psychoanalyze a sin, and sometimes it can be a great harm to ignore a symptom.

Basilea Schlink (1972) said it is not sin itself that is the important thing, but rather, it is our attitudes toward our sin. If one keeps it to oneself, in one's heart, either out of indifference or out of discouragement, one opens oneself up into a fruit of hell. If one brings one's sin to Jesus, confesses it before men, she says then it can be blotted out through grace.

Bitterness and irreconcilability are the result of not forgiving. If we don't reconcile ourselves with others we start to mistrust, become quarrelsome, repress our thoughts or acts in order to cope, and end up bearing the consequences.

In the story of the fall of man, Adam and Eve were "one" before the fall. They felt no shame because they did not experience each other as strangers, separate individuals. After the fall there was estrangement, indicated by their need to cover their nakedness. Eve did not try to protect Adam nor did he defend her, but he tried to avoid punishment by denouncing her. Their sin was to treat each other as separate, isolated, selfish human beings who couldn't overcome their separation in the act of loving union. We try to overcome separateness by submission, domination, or by trying to silence awareness and reason.

Kierkegaard (1854) says sin is to be in despair, unwilling to be oneself before God. For him, the opposite of sin is not virtue but faith. If we look at the teachings of Jesus in healing situations, we see this theme come through: "Your sins are forgiven. Your faith has made you whole."

2. Foreign Land

Some of the passages that man goes through in search of harmony are seen in the story of Moses called to lead the Israelites. This story is found in the Book of Exodus in the Old Testament.

The Israelites became too numerous and strong in Egypt after Joseph's death, so Egypt needed to take steps against their increased power. Egypt's solution was to wear the Israelites down by being slave drivers. What happened during this time? The Israelites increased in number under the oppression. They found reward in having children. Haven't we seen this happen in history? We look at our country—the slaves, the poor, the oppressed—and we see things haven't changed that much. (In Africa, in some of their cultures, the wife with the most children still has the most status in the hierarchy of the wife kingdom.) When there is an oppression, there is an inner drive that needs to be expressed.

The pharaoh of Egypt demanded all boy babies be killed. One baby, Moses, was hidden by his mother. He spent three of his critical developmental months loved and cared for by his mother. His basic roots were developing. When he was three months old, his mother placed him in a basket and put it in the Nile. The pharaoh's daughter found Moses and favored him. It just so happened that Moses' mother was found and asked to nurse him. Moses then spent his early formative years with his mother, his own heritage.

Then Moses was brought up and trained by the pharaoh's Egyptian leaders. Yet he was different. One day he saw an Egyptian strike a Hebrew slave. Moses killed the Egyptian for the cruelty inflicted upon a brother. He lived in fear of being killed if the pharaoh learned of the murder. This is the first adult transition period in Moses' life when he realized he was a *stranger in a foreign land.*

These are the formative years of a man whom God called to lead His people. He called Moses first into the midst of strangers in a foreign land. Abraham (Genesis 12) was called to go to a strange land away from his family. He, in his old age, left his family and went to a foreign land, not knowing what was ahead of him except a call from his God.

Jesus had a similar beginning to that of Moses. Herod had requested the killing of all boy babies. His father, Joseph, had to escape to a foreign land with Jesus. Jesus said, " . . . a man's foes will be those in his own household" (Matt. 10:35). Is he saying that possibly we must separate from our family, if not physically at least psychologically, to become more creative and develop as individuals?

One other instance (Genesis 37) is Joseph. He was sold as a slave by his envious brothers. He lived in a strange land with foreigners and developed into a great leader and saved his people.

We also must make a transition in our early adulthood to break off from our family and go to a *foreign land* in which we will struggle to become who we are to be. To deal with going into this foreign land, whether psychological or physical, brings possible fears. Risk is involved. There are possible changes, burdens, pains, joys, enlightenment that takes place. Jung (1933) described this process as a development into self. We will refer to it as a development into *wholeness.*

Abraham (Genesis 12), when called into a strange land, feared being destroyed. He lied about Sarah being his wife, saying she was his sister because he thought this would protect his own life. In the journey of life, there may be fears and doubts as to whether we're on the right path. There was a trust for Abraham that came, but yet fear lingered.

Joseph (Genesis 39), when confronted by the pharaoh's wife's lies, was put in prison. This instance shows us that in this foreign land we may be confronted with a choice between values. The consequences of our choice may cause us to be imprisoned for a period of time. We will be rejected, and our growth may seem to be stunted. In looking back, we may find real values to be learned through the pain and struggle.

Today this may be more difficult for us. We are growing up without our values being as obvious as they were in the past. Parents are confused as to what they value, and the young are confused in return by not seeing real values. We are saying one thing and living another. We're living in a time when traditions no longer hold, either in practice or in being respected. Some children were interviewed on TV. They were asked about telling lies. They said their parents lie all the time. Mom will tell them to tell someone she is not there when the phone rings. Their parents lie on the phone to people when they call. They said their parents tell them they shouldn't lie but then they themselves do. The children all felt it was okay to lie. For them the problem was, how much they should lie.

Frankl (1967) says meaning must be found not given, discovered rather than invented. He speaks of three chief values we each may experience: experiential, creative, and attitudinal. Experiential is usually for the young, creative for the middle-aged, and attitudinal for the aged; but they might apply to all depending on how one takes one's losses and changes in life. Frankl (1967) tells of an experience he had in the Nazi concentration camp. Men who came from the same environment behaved differently. The choices they made prepared them to be either saints or swine. He saw it as a matter of their choice and ability to look beyond their present circumstances.

Tilden Edwards (1977) states that our basic attitude is most important. He states just as we do not wait for God but God, so we do not wait for but on others. We have chosen willfully to act, not to dependently wait for God or others to do the action and work for us.

Those closest to us remain surprisingly mysterious. If we think we know others and their needs perfectly, our service is likely to be oppressive. We will act out of our own assumption and give others what we think they need. This, more than likely, may be only a projection of our own needs. Our greatest service to others is to give them "space," to provide an environment that frees their spirits to unfold and their bodies to heal. The environment doesn't *make* healing happen; rather it *allows* it to happen. All we can do is to be patiently attentive; watching, being open for the way love might come forth through us in a situation.

In this foreign land, Moses killed the foreigner who confronted his Hebrew brother (Exodus 2:11-22). Jung talks about the two sides of us. He sees one as the foreigner or the *shadow*. The other side is the *persona* or the conscious side of us; it is the part that we can identify with. The shadow is the unconscious part that we may not be aware of but which affects us. We don't want to believe it, and we try to reject it. We see it as our enemy. In our dreams we run away from it. The shadow may be that part we project onto someone else; a characteristic in someone else that we react to strongly.

We may attempt to kill the foreign part of us that is confronting the basic roots of our life. If we succeed in killing it, we may experience anxiety and want to flee, as Moses did. Jung calls us to deal with this negative element and allow the positive value of that relationship to be integrated within us. If we don't, guilt and fear will enslave us. We fear that the rooted part of us will poison us if we don't attack and kill it first (Sanford, 1978).

When Jesus (Matthew 4) was going to the foreign land, He was willing to accept that part of life. He did not kill the negative side, but He certainly confronted the evil and attempted to integrate the opposites to bring harmony within. It was painful! It meant confronting Satan in the wilderness. It meant being willing to risk confronting and having values that He saw as more lasting than temporal values of wealth, glory, and power. He did not kill or go off the deep end. He saw the life He wanted, which was more than for Himself alone and His own glory. It was for him to put utter dependency on God, humble Himself, and obey God's will. In all these instances, there was a choice made. One thing that happened was that Jesus lost his life for this growth to wholeness. He lost his physical life and gained life anew.

We also must lose the I, *ego*, the conscious part, letting down the masks that are hidden behind the I, so that real growth can take place in us and also through us. This, we see, can involve pain, fear, conflicts of values. It must involve cutting the umbilical cord between parents and children. It must, in most cases, involve losing the life as we presently live in order to find real meaning. This part of the journey is difficult for us to accept or want because we would rather many times live with the pain and situation we're now in instead of moving on. The unknown is fearful, and the acceptance we get from others for where we are now may be rewarding enough. If we grow and mature beyond a present situation, the support from others may not be there. Do we dare to journey in the foreign land? Do we have a choice?

3. The Call

After we're called to go into the foreign land, the next transition is the *call to be.* Moses (Exodus 3:1-6) saw the bush burning but yet not being consumed. He said he must go check out this strange sight and see why it was burning. What would you have done? Then a voice called from the middle of the bush, "Moses, Moses."

Moses answered, "Here I am."

God responded, "Take off your shoes, for you are on holy ground. I am the God of your father, the God of Abraham, Isaac and Jacob."

God was showing Moses his roots, his identity. Moses covered his face, afraid to look at God. God then told Moses he was to lead his people out of Egypt to freedom. Moses questioned, "Who, me? Who am I to go to Pharaoh and bring the sons of Israel out of Egypt? Who am I going to say sent me?"

God answered, "Tell them I AM sent me."

Moses, feeling more insecure (wouldn't you with this response?), tried to get out of this situation he had walked into by asking, "What if they don't believe me?"

After God tells Moses He would perform miracles, Moses still came back with a rationalization. "I'm a slow speaker and unable to speak well."

God confronted him, "Who gave man his mouth? Who gave him sight or makes him blind? Who makes him deaf or mute? Go ... 'll tell you what to say."

Finally, God in His anger, told Moses that his brother Aaron would speak for him.

Joseph's call came in a dream (Genesis 37). He saw his father, mother, and brothers bowing down to him. He told his dream to his father and brothers, causing jealousy among his brothers. He did not realize what the significance of the dream was until many years later. He only sensed its impact on his life's direction.

Paul was on the road to Damascus and became blind (Acts 9). A voice said, "Why do you persecute me?" This instance was a turning point in Paul's life. This act awakened him to lead a people he had been persecuting up to that point of his life.

With Samuel, it came in a vision (1 Samuel 3:5). He heard a voice call him, and he thought it was Eli. He ran to Eli. Eli, old in age, said, "I didn't call you go back and lie down." Finally, after the third try, Eli told Samuel the voice was that of Yahweh and to answer him.

These are a few men who have heard and answered the call of God. They kept their eyes on God. If they had looked at themselves, they would have fallen. These men were inspired to a task and not to an honor. Life is not what a person wants to do, but what his God meant for him to do. For every person God has a plan. No one life is purposeless. Scripture reveals God has chosen each of us for a special task. It is not for self-glory and pride but for service, humility, and love for men.

This call brings out something else, the importance of silence. Silence, as a simple rule, can be very, very fruitless, but silence as the way in which we listen together to our God's presence in our midst is an indispensable element in a healthy community life. It opens us up to guidance. Much emphasis is placed on words in the form of conferences, study days, and sharing sessions. However, it seems to underline a realization that words can only bear fruit when they are born out of silence. Especially in periods of crisis, conflict and strong emotional tensions, silence can offer not only healing but also show new ways to enjoy our lives together.

The call comes while a person is in solitude. Henri Nouwen (1979) says our world is in a state of emergency, and fear elevating anger has a powerful focus in human behavior. People are driven together by fear and band together in anger. He suggests that solitude is the place wherein a response to the emergencies of our time can be made, hearing the inner call, where we can rediscover our common vocation.

In more psychological terms, we can again look at Frankl or Jung, especially in examining the inner voice and direction people receive in dreams and visions. Frankl (1975) referred to the *unconscious God* as man's relationship to a God who Himself is hidden. Frankl says the unconscious only relates to the Divine. The unconscious is not the Divine, nor does it possess attributes of the Divine. The unconscious lacks omniscience. This force operating in man through the unconscious is profoundly personal. He sees his relationship with the unconscious God as a personal decision, while Jung (1933) sees it as an instinctive drive or archetypical process occurring in a person.

The Biblical concept is that we hear the call by the inner voice of Yahweh calling. When His miraculous power is released through us there is a hardening of our hearts and others around us. We may rationalize that it is nothing special. We may say that it is no real sign. Our hearts then become hardened and we are no longer willing to listen, to see . . . we experience the Pharaoh of our lives. We may become bugged and bothered too much, and then in desperation cry out, "Let it be God's way." Things may get better, and then we have a change of heart again. This Power that is greater than ourselves makes our hearts hard, because we want to control and make sure we have things under our own control.

Fromm (1968) says that a child starts life with faith in goodness, love, and justice. He has faith in his mother or any other person close to him. It can be expressed as faith in God.

For many children this faith is shattered at an early age. Each takes these losses differently. Many times the person remains skeptical, hopes for a miracle to restore his faith, and tests people by throwing himself into the arms of a powerful authority.

Fromm states we have a choice as to repress or move forward. We can become fully human and regain our lost harmony. We have the choice and the longer we continue to make wrong decisions, the more our hearts harden; the more we make right decisions, the more our hearts soften and we become alive. In the process of choosing, we are in the act of freeing ourselves. In the process the degree of our capacity to make choices varies with each act. Each step in life that increases my self-confidence, my integrity, my courage, my conviction also increases my capacity to choose desirable alternatives, until it becomes more difficult for me to choose the undesirable. On the other hand, each act of surrender and cowardice weakens me, opens the path for more acts of surrender, and eventually freedom is lost.

Hardening of the heart or the blocking of the freedom of choice can be done at a young age when a child desires to do one thing and is bribed by the parent to do the other. He takes the parent's choice and represses his own need. Each bribe after this reinforces the way of life until the heart becomes hardened to freedom (unable to choose). His awareness is dulled by these prior choices that are now unconscious.

If a person becomes indifferent to life, there is no longer any hope that he can choose the good for his life. If the heart becomes so hardened to the entire human race or to its most powerful members, then the life of mankind may be extinguished at the very moment of its greatest promise. When the heart is hardened, an inner weakness and lack of self-confidence increases.

Fromm (1968) gave an example of the hardening process. A little boy played with the family maid's son. The mother, for social reasons, bribed him by taking him to get candy if he didn't play with the undesirable boy. As the lad grew older, he fell in love with a gal across the tracks. The parents, not wanting him to marry her, told him they would send him to Europe for a six-month vacation. While in Europe he forgot his fiancée and when he came back, the mold was set. His father wanted him to become a doctor like himself, even though the boy's interest was in engineering. He followed his father's desire and didn't listen to his "inner call." At mid-life he will still be seeking power and other means of satisfaction to compensate for the inner potential he never satisfied. He will have become hardened to his own uniqueness before God.

In Biblical times the Egyptians' punishment rained down and not without warning because of their hardened hearts. They suffered from their crimes since they harbored such bitter hatred toward strangers, making slaves of their guests and benefactors, the Israelites. They first welcomed them with feasting and equal rights, then afflicted them with forced labor. The Egyptians then were struck with many plagues.

These plagues strike us today. In our own lives, we open up part of our existence to strangers. We may rejoice over such relationships. Then we start to possess, enslave others in that relationship. We may have warnings, but we may ignore them and be plagued. The Egyptians thirsted because they were not able to drink the water that had turned to blood. We also are plagued with a thirst, one for the water of life. We become plagued by our instincts—a plague of frogs. We don't take heed and those instincts die. We become bugged, bitter, and emotionally drained—the plague of mosquitos. We become plagued by the loss of strength, the means for energy—or "live stock" of life. Physically we are attacked and then the original youth of our life is killed—the plague of death of the first child. Darkness for man sets in at this point, the plague of darkness.

These drastic situations can be overcome by each being open to his unique inner call. We must allow our children this freedom, as Jacob did for Joseph and Eli for Samuel. We need to accept that still small voice and our own intuition in order to realize meaning and direction in our lives. We must be ready to say, "Yes, I hear and trust," then to move forward, boldly trusting that there is a purpose for our life. Our path ahead is preparing us for our task. Joseph's path was a rough road, but he endured to accomplish his goal. He was enslaved for seventeen years, but he finally served his people.

4. A Covenant

Astrange thing happened after Moses received his call. Moses was on his journey back home and halted for the night. Yahweh came to meet him and tried to kill him (Exodus 4:24-26). Moses was being attacked because he was uncircumcised. Circumcision was part of the covenant between God and Abraham for all Israelites. Moses had accepted his call without his part of the deal being fulfilled. Through this episode, we see one man's responding to an unusual situation, questioning his capability and strength, and then after being given assurance and support, forgetting his part of the package the covenant to his God.

Jacob had a similar situation of struggling with God (Genesis 32:26-29). He had his hip dislocated as he wrestled. Jacob would not let God go until He blessed him. Jacob's name was changed to Israel because he had been strong with God, and God promised he would prevail against men. This name changing is prevalent throughout scripture. Sarai, Abraham's wife, was changed to Sarah. Saul was changed to Paul. Names are changed today for many when they make a covenant with another in marriage, business, or upon graduation.

In the development of the clown (Sanford, 1979), the concept is developed of removing the masks. In the whiting out of the face, a new birth takes place. One discovers and retains a new name. This name is born out of weeks of struggle to discover that part of Self that is seeking to be expressed.

These views of the covenant may seem trivial to man today. Jung (1964) talks of the *archetype* of man in the same vein as the Biblical covenant. We search for identity and in the search discover our roots, the special historical wants that are a model for all mankind. These are the archetype. Each generation asks, 'Who are we?" We might consider the Bible as the story of God trying to create a people for Himself through a covenant with a solitary people known as Israel. Through this relationship of God in proximity with them came the possibility for all nations to acquire their true identity (Boelter, 1971). Scripture strongly reminds us that God's plan and purpose in the covenant will not be known by an attempt to explore the nature of God through the use of our minds. However, we can plot the boundaries of His nature.

A covenant was made between God and Abraham (Genesis 15:7). Abraham took animals and severed them. Then a ball of fire passed between the severed animals. This was to signify God's covenant to Abraham, that he was to inherit the land God promised. In a covenant, if a party was unfaithful to the agreement that was made, that party was like a dead animal.

Today, the covenant is symbolically expressed in a marriage ceremony. This is a *call to commitment*, which is one of Erikson's (1964) developmental tasks of man. We seek for identity today. There is emphasis today on being an individual and doing your own thing. In response to a call to be a whole person, such as Moses, we see a response to a covenant. This is a call to a commitment to be obedient and trusting toward the other party.

When Moses finally accepted his call and commitment to lead his people out of Egypt, he did falter in his trust even when he knew the sea was before him and the advancing hosts were behind him. There was no visible way to escape. He led his people to the very edge of the water. He had done his task. He had to go to the edge, and His God did the rest. So it is with us that we must go forward even though we can't see how to get across the barrier ahead; we must keep going, the waters will divide, and we will also walk through the midst of the sea on dry land.

Should we encourage people to risk an inner call and move ahead to the very edge of the water? Should we try to get in tune with our inner voice?

5. Wilderness Experience

We accept the call and all looks rosy at the start. We are led to believe today that if one has found one's niche in life, then one should have smooth sailing. We hear in advertisements about the easy life. We read books explaining how to attain this utopia. The bookshelves are being loaded with books with catchy titles about how to find our dream. A person of God sometimes feels he should be free from suffering and then when it is not clear and smooth grumbles.

When we do not obtain this peace, then we have failed and start to grumble. We sense we're on the wrong path, have made the wrong decision, and should turn around. We feel there must be a better way.

So it was with the Israelites. No sooner had the people gotten out of slavery than they started complaining of thirst, hunger, and risks of war Exodus 15). Their souls were resisting growth. Their doubts and fears drove them back into the wilderness again. Yahweh warned the Israelites when He gave them the Ten Commandments that they were to reject the idols and the horrors that would attack them (Exodus 20). The first three commandments deal with man's relationship to God. The last seven deal with man's relationship with human beings. The Israelites were not to pollute their minds with the idols of Egypt because God had brought them out of Egypt. Not one listened to God.

We also, when we're released from bondage and find freedom, may rebel against giving up past horrors and idols. We become blind with doubts and fears, which drive us further into the wilderness. We must keep conquering and overcoming obstacles in life. The path is not always clear ahead. The goal is not obtaining more material goods than needed. The goal is not to get more for me. The people's problem seemed to increase the more they focused on self. The people had not learned to conquer their own emotional outbursts, their own selfish desires, but yet they wanted to control God and others.

A strong example of one who achieved self-conquest is Jesus Christ. He was mocked before the soldiers, struck, spat upon, and answered not a word. By the power of perfect silence, perfect self-control, can we prove the right to govern? We are each so complex, so different, actuated by different motives, controlled by different circumstances, influenced by different suffering. How can we judge another?

In the wilderness, the Israelites were impatiently waiting on the promise and message of God. They threw their jewels into the fire collectively to build an idol to worship. Shame was upon them. God let nothing go unchecked, punishing the fathers' faults in the sons and in the grandsons to the third and fourth generations (Exodus 34:7). We build worthless idols from our jewels, and our children end up with a sense of no real value. We then experience, as Frankl (1967) says, an *existential vacuum*, which is a sense of emptiness, futility, and feeling of frustration and inferiority. As with the Israelites, a man neither knows what he must do nor what he should do. He ends up doing what others wish him to do; he conforms and throws his jewels in the fire. We have been reduced to complex biochemical mechanisms, the naked ape.

De Castillijo (1973) tells how we hunger for life and then try to live through our children the life we failed to live ourselves. This puts a terrible burden upon the children, making them live out the unused talents or unconscious desires of their parents. De Castillijo tells how in T. S. Eliot's *Family Reunion*, the son, Harry, pushed his wife overboard without really meaning to do so, and only later discovered that he had carried out his father's unadmitted desire to get rid of his own wife. All but Harry thought it was an accident.

His illustration was used to point out how the sins of the fathers are visited upon the children unto the fourth generation. The real tragedy is the failure of being aware of the prospect when one is capable of forestalling it (De Castillio, 1973, 119-20).

As individuals we each must be willing to look to our historical background. Each will be from a different perspective. Our parents pass on to us their darkness, as well as their richness and light. Only in looking back, having more respect for our inner lives, can we stop this darkness from being passed on to the next generation and live more fully ourselves.

Thomas's (1978) bi/polar theory can help us focus on more creative use of our strengths or become more conscious of our capabilities. Thomas's theory stresses man's strengths and how he uses these strengths as tools in relationships and interpersonal behavior. These bi/polar strengths are styles or strengths that enable people to function in the world. These strengths are perceived in pairs and stand at opposite ends of a common bipolar dimension. The two strengths in each pair are referred to as polar strengths. These pairs can conceivably be creative when used together.

One main pair of strengths is the thinking/risking strength. Some of us are greater risk-takers, while others are more given to thought. Neither strength is better than the other. When one defensively uses one strength or tends to overstress it until it controls him, we might say he could be entering into a wilderness experience. He has then a tendency to experience despair and hopelessness. It is similar to the use of defense mechanisms commonly referred to in psychoanalysis. Thomas says the person then has become *polarized*, using one strength to the extreme. Where it has gone beyond the point of being creative, it becomes destructive to the person using it and also to people around him.

Another tool developed today is the *Enneagram*. This process is to help us investigate the rich and challenging approach to holiness and self-discovery. At one level it can be seen as a personality theory. It is essentially a spirituality of conversion. It assumes that spirituality and the human journey are integrally linked. Again, it is a tool to create an awareness within us of whom we are and how we relate to God and man.

Back to Moses in the wilderness. He sent the leaders to spy on a new land, a land flowing with milk and honey (Numbers 13:25-32). Only one of those who came back said they were able to go up against the people there. Others saw the people stronger than themselves and saw themselves as grasshoppers. They gave evil reports of the land. They rationalized and didn't trust their Lord. They stayed in the wilderness, grumbling about their condition, wanting to return to slavery. Their faithlessness again caused suffering to their children. The children could not get out of the wilderness until their parents died.

How many times do we see situations out of perspective, see the giants of life, and then retreat to the wilderness? We fear to risk to get beyond the wall that divides us from entering the new land, the land flowing with milk and honey. We have not the faith and inner trust to see that we're not grasshoppers, but people who are given the strength to move out of the wilderness of life. In retreat, we feel more secure. We'd rather choose our slavery, our misery, and die in it, than risk living in a land that offers freedom. Oh, if we'd only confront our lives! Are we willing to grow, expand our lives, giving opportunities to our family, our community through risks for a better and new land?

In the wilderness we tend to let defense mechanisms spring forth. We may rationalize the giants of life. We may regress as the Israelites, wanting to go back to slavery. We may repress, not remembering the prior hardship and not seeing the past slavery. We may project onto our children unfulfilled dreams. We deny the opportunities that come, denying that the land is filled with milk and honey. We may become fixed in a certain stage of development. The Israelites got stuck in one stage of their development and to move forward caused them great anxiety. The Israelites used displacement. They directed their energy to the golden calf when they did not have Moses to instruct them.

Our ego-defense mechanisms may hoodwink us. Even though they may help keep down the anxiety, they distort reality or deny it. This hinders growth to a fulfilling life. We then become enslaved, stagnate, and are like grasshoppers meeting the giants.

PART II

CALL TO WHOLENESS

We have seen thus far that every man and woman becomes a whole person in his /her own unique way. Jesus had said the gate to life is a "narrow way" (Matthew 7:13). We need to walk through the gate as we are guided and not seek it by collective suggestion. Many times what happens is that we merge unconsciously with each other in the community. We feel at one with each other and then emerge as a group personality. This may become destructive because we may not develop the inner potential that is needed for us as individuals and as a community.

6. RUNNING AWAY

We turn now to the story of Jonah to help illustrate what could happen when we are not honest with ourselves and have chosen the wrong attitude for life. We will look at one man's experience in trying to run away from an inner call. We will see how he inhibited growth for himself and tried to stunt others because of his own dishonesty with himself.

Jonah, upon receiving a call from God, ran to Tarshish. Tarshish represented the end of the world. God had asked him to go to Nineveh to tell the people that their wickedness had become known to Him. Jonah instead ran about as far as he could from Yahweh.

Our first reaction to the call may be to get as far away as possible. We may also not want to take the responsibility for a change in our life or the life of another whom we cannot consciously control completely. It requires giving up more and more ego consciousness, the "I," to the will of God. We cling and don't let go. We find many excuses. One key symbol is the running away found in dreams, the running from self. We perceive the pursuer as our enemy, but yet he's our friend. No secrets are hidden or nothing missed by the seeing eye of God.

Jonah gets in trouble over his flight. We get in trouble also because ours affects our development into wholeness. These disturbances coming forth from the flight can be registered and emerge in the form of anxiety. We fear the return of the repressed. Second, there may emerge a great depression, which is the surest way to force us out of the old path of life and get us beyond it. If the disturbance is great enough, it can cause psychosis. The ego can't control it because it comes forth too quickly from the unconscious. The unconscious is demanding recognition at all costs. People can get through this call to wholeness with even the deepest pain. We need to look at them not with labels and clinically but as persons with *inward pain*. If we treat them thus, their inward pain may begin to heal.

This disturbance can even be experienced physically. If this happens, then we must get it out of the body and back into the psyche in order to deal with it.

Jonah got on a boat to get to Tarshish. By going to Tarshish, he thought he could become invisible to God. We also want to become invisible to God. We either don't get involved or we don't let our real feelings come out. If one wants to become real, then real problems must emerge and be dealt with creatively.

The *inner self* operates through relationship. Sooner or later other individuals won't stand for a person trying to be invisible and he will be confronted.

7. Storm of Life

Jonah got caught in a great storm at sea. The ship threatened to break up. This is the state in which our *ego* begins to collapse. The violent storm is the anger of God. We live out the personification of another and then the storm comes within.

Jonah knew better. He was a prophet. He knew there was something special about his life. Once a person has this relationship with life, he can't get away from it. Once growth to wholeness starts, you can't regress. The *self* or *inner self* won't tolerate it. Jesus said, "Once the hand is laid on the plough, no one who looks back is fit for the kingdom of God" (Luke 9:62).

This growth to wholeness makes heroes out of us. Once you see something, you can't deny that you've seen it.

The storm of life is God speaking to us in a loud voice. It is much better for us if He can speak in a small voice. A nightmare comes when God has to shout. Dreaming is one way to listen to the small voice of God speaking.

The sailors took fright in the storm, and Jonah went down in the hole and fell asleep. The sailors are the good guys, the positive attitudes. They are the people who find it sufficient to work at something honestly. We need this for wholeness. They find the right slot in life and are honest about it.

At an inner level, they are our basic ordinary humanity, which if we let them, they will always try to help us out. They are the common and ordinary parts of life and should be respected. The sailors threw cargo overboard and called in their gods. We do everything that is expected of us, as they did. We buy a new car, a new home, calling in our gods to calm the storm. The sailors had to do something else to stop the raging storm, but they didn't know what. The problem was Jonah. He fell asleep.

When Jesus was at Gethsemene, his disciples, Peter, James, and John, fell asleep. They were unconscious of Jesus' suffering or psychologically their egos were as fast asleep as Jonah was unconscious to the violent storm. As Jesus released his will to God the disciples slept. The *inner self* is like a vessel being filled from the *Unconscious God*, and the *ego* must not fall asleep to its transforming power.

The boat's captain came upon Jonah and told him to call upon his God. Jonah was affecting them by the state he was in. We tend to forget how we affect other people by who we are and what state we're in. A person who starts on the path to wholeness of life starts to affect others around him, especially those who have not started to mature into a more wholesome life.

Because of relationship with the *inner self*, people are either attracted to a person or they crucify him. He will be someone people will remember in a very special way. Jesus is an example of a person who affected others because of his relationship with *Self*. He was crucified. Lincoln was another man who in his maturity and growth to wholeness was crucified.

The sailors wanted to draw lots to see who had brought on this evil. Someone was out of relationship with God. God brought evil to them but also good to them. When the ego goes against the inner self, it causes the dark evil side of *self* to come out. This can be very destructive. Attitudes in our own consciousness that are unworthy God will try to destroy.

The lot fell upon Jonah. He could no longer be the invisible man. The questions began to come. Tension became greater and greater. We must have a healthy respect for any nightmare that emerges. If we refuse to, they can cause darkness in our lives and destroy us. "The fear of the Lord is the beginning of wisdom; fools spurn wisdom and discipline" (Proverb 1:7). '"Wisdom? It is fear of the Lord. Understanding? Avoidance of evil" (Job 28:28).

The sailors threw Jonah in the sea and offered sacrifice to Yahweh. Jonah told them they must throw him in the sea. Jonah was a psychologically sound person and knew what they must do to calm the waves. After trying other things, the only choice the sailors had remaining was to get rid of Jonah and his psychological honesty, the essential ingredient for salvation.

When Jacob was about to cheat his father (with his mother Rebecca's help) for Esau's birthright, he said, "He may perceive my cheating him" (Genesis 27:12). Jacob was rationalizing for the act of cheating. Rationalization may be a means used for psychological honesty.

8. DEPTHS OF SUFFERING

Jonah stayed in the belly of a great fish. *Great fish* is a symbol of *Self*. This image is what Jung (1964) calls an *archetypal* image. It represents a very important event that happens over and over again. Jonah experienced the *Self* negatively. He gets integrated and swallowed up by it. There are three possible consequences. We can use artificial means to get out of it, by using pills, etc., and then go on as before, except in a more regressive way of living. We can avoid it and go back to life as prior but slightly inferior to before. Second, we can get sick and stay sick. Third, we can become enlightened by it through conscious effort and then we will give more enlightened service to others (Sanford, 1979).

Many healers experience this, even becoming very sick and being at what they feel is the end and then becoming healed. Then they have received the gift of healing. They must maintain this gift or become sick again (Sanford, 1977).

Jonah really suffered. He went into a rage, saying that he might as well be dead as to go on living. He had to suffer to be cured of his wrong attitude. The only way to grow is through suffering unless we heed the still small voice. We often have a wrong attitude about illness, unaware that anxiety and depression can help us understand the illness. They cause us to deal with the inner voice and what is keeping us from wholeness.

What is ill is in the ego. Suffering is the inevitable consequence of the meeting of the ego and the Self. They both suffer. Self suffers because it is limitless, but to incarnate itself with the ego, it must succumb to the finite. The ego suffers because it will be wounded by the Self (Sanford, 1979).

Christ is a good example of what happens when the ego and Self meet. His ego suffered to the point of crucifixion. Not until death was the Self again able to be expressed fully in the resurrection.

Suffering need not be pointless unless we lose our child-likeness. Jesus said, "Except ye become as little children . . . and humble yourself as this little child ... shall ye enter the kingdom of heaven" (Matthew 18). We need to find the correct attitude.

Jonah prays. In praying he is relating the ego to the *Unconscious God* and his own inner being. He begins to get out of the dark state. In the depressed state, he thinks about God most. He centers his Self on God. If a person hates God, he could think more about God as one who loves Him.

9. REBIRTH

We can't tell when this moment will come. We can only persist and have a right attitude. By Jonah's being vomited up, God gave him a second chance. This rebirth is not all beautiful. With the rebirth came God's call a second time to go to Nineveh. This call or force does not want to do Jonah in but just wants to be recognized. As long as the *Self* can relate to the ego, wholeness can take place. We may get many choices to respond, but sooner or later, we will run out of chances. Yahweh told Jonah to go up to Nineveh; Jonah still dragged his feet.

Jonah goes there as a hero. He is a prophet, and the people of Nineveh don't know God. He had a superior consciousness and he must live up to it. If you achieve a superior life, then you must live up to that life. Jonah's message was that in forty more days, Nineveh could be destroyed. He went and preached only half the message that Yahweh addressed to him. He was supposed to inform them of their wickedness and Yahweh's love. If they turned to Him, they would be saved. Jonah didn't want the people to be saved. He didn't like them. He acted like the man who hasn't accepted what Jung calls the shadow side or the dark side of himself and was projecting it on the people.

The dark side of ourself that we are unaware of, we project onto others. We can project the positive as well as the negative. When this projection goes on, it stunts our development to wholeness of life. This will preclude relationships. Jonah was not willing to forgive because he had projected his negative side on them. When we aren't projecting, we can hear and understand where others are. Jesus said make peace with your adversary while you are on the way with him (Matthew 5:25).

We have to come to terms with the dark side. Jonah should have asked, "Why do I hate them?" The people had started to understand God. They did not try to rationalize their old way of living. They were out in the open about it. They lost their persona and removed their masks. They fasted and wore sackcloth. We can't remove masks in private when locked up. We must stand in naked reality before someone (Sanford, 1978).

Jonah was in a great rage. He felt he might as well be dead as to go on living. Yahweh is loving, merciful, and relenting. He implies if we don't connect up to Him, there could be a judgmental obstacle.

Jung might have said Jonah was having an "anima attack." The *anima* is the feminine side of man. It is moody, sullen, withdrawn, and the part that is in a fog (Sanford, 1978). Jonah had been transformed into a vague, moody type of man. He had rejected the feminine side of himself. This is the portion of the self-involving feeling, loving, and friendliness. The anima then undermined Jonah. Jung (1964) says the anima (feminine side) intensifies, methodizes, exaggerates, falsifies our emotional tone in relationships. Everything becomes a big deal. This is usually caused by a personal slight or hurt. The person, not having the skills to deal with it, lets the hurt feelings become repressed. The anima rises to force expression of the repressed hurt. The person must be able to express "I'm feeling angry with what you did." With this skill, he can deal with moods creatively (Sanford, 1978).

Jonah didn't deal with his mood creatively. He felt rejected by God. He had done more for God than these people, and he saw these people as strangers and unworthy. God was favoring these people. Jonah said to God, "Look at me! You haven't given me as much. You love them more than me."

Yahweh asks, "Are you right to be angry?" A dialogue emerges between God and Jonah. This dialogue again is a example of Frankl's (1975) *Unconscious God* talking to the conscious. This dialogue in a relationship is not dumping on

The ego must live in reality and with real facts, but the *Self* doesn't. The inner reality demands something that the outer reality can't deal with. God asks Jonah a consciousness-raising question: "Are you right to be angry?"

Then Jonah went east of the city and sat under a castor-oil plant. Worms attacked the plant. Jonah withdrew to his inner mood and became a little boy feeling sorry for himself.

Jonah must suffer more. The first time he had to suffer in the belly of the great fish. Now Jonah could have gotten out of this by saying, "I'm tired of this bad mood." He doesn't have to be in this mood. He could choose not to be. Frankl (1965) would say that we could aim at *de-reflection* or not putting so much emphasis on the situation or instead of being overbearing toward ourselves with so much self-reflection and self-observation. Man has the freedom to move "from what" he is being driven toward "what is" his responsibility—doing something transcendent and beyond self.

God tried to get Jonah out of his reflection. There was hope because Jonah answered God that he had a right to be angry. Now he could get beyond his helplessness. When one feels hopeless, one can commit suicide. One throws oneself into total despair. Jonah was angry and did not see that God was being just. Jonah said, "You love the people of Nineveh more than me." God said, "You are only upset about the castor-oil plant, which cost you no labor, which you did not make grow, which sprouted in a night and has perished in a night. And am I not to feel sorry for Nineveh, the great city, in which there are more than a hundred and twenty thousand people who cannot tell their right hands from their left, to say nothing at all of the animals" (Jonah 4:10-11).

We also see that God was concerned about the animals. Animals are truly precious in nature. They are part of God's kingdom, and we can't afford to let them be destroyed. Animals represent our own natural instincts. We are to make them our friends. In fairy tales they play the roles of heroes.

God tried to get Jonah to get to the bottom of his anger. This giant anger is a rage that can eat up everything. It can be a cold rage, as when a sniper sits by the roadside and shoots at people. There is a more human rage, which gets at the heart of the matter.

We carry around with us hurt feelings and sick emotions. Feelings must be expressed. Anger is the number one problem today. We are unwilling to take risks to express it. Our ancestors expressed it on battlefields. For us today, it is an inner battle. When we get in touch with anger, we then get in touch with love. We can't block one emotion without blocking all of them (O'Conner, 1979).

The Book of Jonah ends quickly. It doesn't go on because we haven't gone on in our own growth. Only in our dialogue with God can it go on.

The book ends with God's mercy on all creatures. He had mercy on Jonah in the great fish, on the repentant Nineveh, on Jonah in his self-pity. He is concerned for men and children who can't tell their right hand from their left. It prepares us for the revelation that God is love and in the growth to *wholeness*, there is love. We are to grasp this reality in our journey of life.

PART III

COMMUNITY DEVELOPMENT

Scripture speaks of man being called to a community to serve others. We are not called to build just our lives individually, but to love our neighbors, going to visit the needy, the sick, the ones who are hurting (Matthew 25:33-37).

In the community we are called to bring forth certain qualities. One of these qualities is that of the stronger brother in helping to serve the weaker brother. We are to uphold him (Bonhoeffer, 1954).

10. FAITH

One of our qualities is faith. In Mark 2:1-5, there is a parable of the paralytic, a helpless man who could not walk. This man probably was an outcast because of his illness. There was a concurrent group who believed so strongly that this man, Jesus, could help the paralytic that they came to seek Him. Four men carried the paralytic to Jesus, fighting through the crowd, cutting a hole in the roof, and lowering the man to Jesus. When Jesus saw the four men's faith, he said to the young man, "Your sins are forgiven." The young man walked.

Sometimes in our own life, we may each become a paralytic. When that comes we may be filled with doubts, self-pity, resentment, anger, and a weak faith. Even if we know there is a God who loves us, we can't seem to cross the gulf between ourselves and God and other persons. At these times it helps to recall the times in our lives when we have been blessed, the times when our Lord was very close, the times in our life when there was meaning. Frankl (1964) found that in the concentration camp, survivors were able to look beyond the present circumstance to find meaning in life. That gave them a will to live.

This parable says more! It says if one doesn't have that faith, then others in his community who are stronger need to support him and bring him into a healing situation. As paralytics, our faith may just dry up. We may cry out and find God appears to be silent. People around us just don't seem to relate to us or hear our needs. We just can't seem to share our real feelings. We can't seem to forgive others. The past may seem to haunt us. Joy and expectation are not a part of life. In Isaiah 43, God's chosen people also had grown tired of God. They had not brought God sacrifices, although God's requests were few. They only presented Him with their faults and problems.

We, as the paralytics, may not believe "the joy of the Lord is our strength." Instead we may withdraw from life. We turn to things such as drugs or alcohol instead of people and God. The more we allow them to control our lives, the less feeling we seem to have about people whom we love. This is an ugly, depressing picture, but the family and the community are there to help share the burden. Jesus gave us a key (Matthew 24:12) when he said, "And because wickedness is multiplied, most men's love will grow cold."

The stronger brother must be able to turn a negative situation into a caring community. In a sense, as Paul had said in Philippians 4:4, "Rejoice in the Lord always. Have no anxiety about anything, but in everything by prayer and supplication with THANKSGIVING let your requests be known to God."

Scripture calls us to reach out in love to one another. We are to let our love be genuine. We are to have love that is building up, a love that is reaching out beyond ourselves to impart a meaning and a purpose to life. With this love we are to be filled with praises to the Lord of our life and for other people. With this love we are to perceive beyond the masks of people. Some masks that people hide behind are social status, occupational status, educational background, racial differences, individual differences. We are called to see them not on the basis of their intellect, financial status, or even physical beauty, but as people with an inner beauty who are lovable and capable of loving.

We are called to see a person with a strength and potential who is capable of growth. We do not all have the same function in the community but these gifts can be used to build us all up, as Paul expressed (1 Corinthians 12), "In the body of Christ, there are many members, but not all with the same function. If one member is hurting the other members suffer. If one member is rejoicing the others share in that joy." Paul warns us that we are not to judge, scoff at the weaker brother, tear down, or put stumbling blocks in the way of the weak. We are to please our neighbor for his good, not our own good.

Light shines through our eyes, our actions and concern for others. This light is turned on when we, the caring community, allow the *Unconscious God's* light to come into our lives. We in turn are to be sensitive to the light in others' eyes. We are to be sensitive to when the light is dimmed by tears and eyes grow cold or hard.

The community is to respect the right of that other person, respecting the right that each man has an able key to his own door. When he has the right key to unlock his door to another, then we are to be ready to come in. We need to be sensitive to that person's feelings and have ears to listen. We need to be slow to speak, choosing words that are not just flowery speech, filled with lot of solutions and advice, or words to put him in his place. Words are not to be judgmental, but to be tuned in to the feeling and need of that person. God does not bless us with brothers and sisters to dominate and control, but as someone to serve and share our Father's love. We may even be called to sacrifice if someone is in need.

The Psalmist says (Psalm 34): "Taste and see that the Lord is good." We can also as a helper trust the Psalmist's word and help others experience joy instead of grief. If Jesus' disciples had trusted His word about His coming crucifixion, they would have experienced joy instead of grief. When tragedy comes, man is called to respond to the power of the *Unconscious God*, trusting that He is more powerful than our tragedy. We are called to respond to our fellow friends needs with joy and not distrust.

11. FORGIVENESS

In the community we are constantly dealing with indifference. Many times these indifferences may be expressed in anger and other times possibly held in. In our transitions of life, we may hit crises that have built up over the years. These crises may not be caused by someone else but by an unexpressed anger or bitterness toward someone else or even ourselves.

Man used to express some of this built-up anger and bitterness by physical work and exertion. He had opportunity to release pressure that today we let turn inward. We are a computerized society, used to pushing buttons. Our wars are not physical fighting, as in prior history. War also is pushing the right button. We end up releasing our pressure accumulated from many instances as if we're a time bomb.

Prior to our mobile society, people also had more opportunity to deal with these problems without seeking professional help. Today, churches do not have confessionals, as they were required to in the past. For many it is a public confession that we read. In confession a person would have the opportunity to admit his wrong or feelings that haunted him. He could "get it off his chest."

Theologian John Cobb (1974) outlined the need for confession in daily life. He said:

> In the ordinary course of events I am not moved to careful and honest self-analysis. When I engage in self-examination in the presence of other persons, I can't free myself from concern as to what they think of me or of what the consequence of my confession may be. When seeking professional help, I find that

the categories through which I am helped to self-understanding deal only with limited aspects of my total being. In church when I join with others in confessing my sins, those sins are too generally stated to force me to more careful self-awareness. It is when I am alone that I can bring all these things together and go beyond them. But, if I think of myself as simply alone, I do not find myself drawn to such painful analysis. As long as I am getting by with others, why should I judge myself more exactingly than they do? It is when I think of myself as being alone before God that traditional Christian self-examination, confession, and repentance make sense to me.

Today there exists a restlessness in man when he does not deal with forgiveness. Man asks John Cobb's question, "Why judge myself more exactingly than they do?" Those inner conflicts will exist, be rationalized, and projected onto others. How many of us think of ourselves as alone before God or look at our life in relationship to a power greater than ourselves? Who helps us with this inner dilemma?

Webster defines *forgive* as giving up resentment and the desire to punish; to stop being angry with; to pardon; giving up all claim to punish or exact penalty for; to overlook, cancel or remit a debt. In the following stories, more precise examples will be developed.

In the Unforgiving Servant (Matthew 18:21-25) story, the servant owed the king a large debt that was completely unpayable and the king forgave him. A fellow servant owed this man a debt that was a trifle compared to the debt he owed the king. The first servant demanded that the man pay the debt immediately or face punishment. The servant had projected onto this man his own unforgiving heart over his own debt. We see an example of demanding standards from others that we're not prepared to fulfill ourselves. Barclay (1976) said men know that forgiveness is a lovely thing but yet in actual practice, it is not forgiveness that sways them, but a bitter heart and the desire for vengeance.

Corrie Ten Boom (1974) gave a graphic illustration of forgiveness that took place in Germany after the war. A man came up to her after a speech. She recognized him as the guard who had helped kill her sister when they were in prison camp. He had just become a Christian and admitted having been a guard in a prison camp. He wanted her forgiveness. He raised his hand to shake hers. She could not bear to raise hers. Hate swept through her. She prayed, "Lord, only You have the strength to make me shake his hand." Her hand raised to his. She experienced a warm flow through her hand and arm that she had never felt before. She said she experienced a flow of love through her physically and a release of freedom. Healing came into her life. She was able to accept a person she had condemned.

In the parable of the prodigal son (Luke 15:11-32), the young son was a pleasure-seeking spendthrift and the older son was super-responsible. The parable emphasizes the forgiving and reconciling power of God, which is exemplified in the father. John Sanford (1970), describing this parable, illustrates the evils of pleasure-seeking and the need to forgive and accept others. It is two halves of one whole personality. He looks at the Jungian construct of the two sides of the person: animus-shadow part of the personality. Sanford says the reconciliation comes when the two brothers within one can become one personality. The prodigal side of oneself that is unconscious is to be accepted if we are the elder brother consciously. The elder brother that is unconscious is to be accepted if we consciously are the pleasure-seeker. When we project either side onto someone else, he becomes a non-person. We place judgment upon him.

Sanford (1978) explains how judgment is different from evaluating others because judgment is final. When we judge someone, we subject him to a blanket condemnation. When we judge him, we are claiming to know the meaning and moral consequence of the other person's life. Judging others rests upon our own unconsciousness. Jesus said, "Do not judge and you will not be judged because the judgments you give are the judgments you will get" (Matthew 7:1-2). We can see in others what we hate in ourselves. That's why our judgment of others seems to return to us. Jesus continued (Matthew 7:5), "Hypocrite! Take the plank out of your own eye first, and then you will see clearly enough to take the splinter out of your brother's eye." Then only we will see clearly enough to not project our enemy, our jealousy, our hatred, our greediness, our wealth, our illnesses and sin onto others.

Another view of forgiveness can be seen in the woman who entered the Pharisee's house where Jesus was having a meal (Luke 7:36 47). She had a bad reputation, and she had heard Jesus would be at the Pharisee's house. Because of her love for Jesus, she came with an alabaster jar of oil. She wept over him and with her hair wiped her tears that fell on his feet.

The Pharisee was shocked and said, "If this man were a prophet, he would know who this woman is and not have anything to do with her." Jesus, knowing his thoughts, pointed out the great debt that had been forgiven her and the great love she showed. He closed with, "For this reason I tell you that her sins, her many sins, must have been forgiven her, or she would not have shown such great love. It is the man who is forgiven little who shows little love" (Luke 7:47). This context demonstrates that the woman showed so much affection because she had so many sins forgiven. There was an acceptance and love that had reached out, transmitting a pardon to this woman, so she was free to love in return.

We are to live intensely, even if it means we can no longer avoid blame. The Pharisee played it safe, sought to remain blameless before God, and was not emotionally involved with life and the "sinner." Pharisees were like the church described in Revelation 3:14-15, neither hot nor cold, but lukewarm. These people had been apathetic. They were rich, increasing in goods and having need of nothing, and yet not knowing how wretched and miserable they really were.

Forgiveness releases us from being bound to the outer life or physical existence. We can get to the inner life of man the soul. It is as Jesus said, "He that loseth his life for my sake shall find it" (Matthew 10:39). Holding on to physical hang-ups has no value if our inner life is destroyed in the process.

Maxwell Maltz (1971) said, "When forgiveness is real, genuine, complete, and forgotten, then it is the scalpel which removes the pus from old emotional wounds, heals them and eliminates scar tissue. Even the act of forgiveness should be forgotten, as well as the wrong which was forgiven. Dwelling upon either facet resurrects the wound you are attempting to cauterize. If you are proud of it, you may be apt to feel the other person owes you something for forgiving him. Forgiveness is not to make us 'good' but so we might be happy. We are not to assume a superior posture over other persons."

We must see the wrong and our own feeling of condemnation as being undesirable rather than desirable. We must get beyond the morbid enjoyment of nursing the wound (as long as we can condemn the other, we can feel superior to him). Maltz stated that true forgiveness came when we could be able to see and emotionally accept that there is and was nothing for us to forgive.

One of the stages of man's growth is the ability to develop an *intimate relationship*. In this stage we see the need for forgiveness so clearly. Yet, we are seeing marriages break up all around us. With this separation comes great bitterness, hatred, and anger. Some never get over the hurt and deep-rooted feelings from this tragic experience even though the marriage may not be the cause of all of the hurts being expressed at the time. If forgiveness could come into the hearts of these broken people, there could be a greater understanding in love at its very depths. It is a love that most of us will never experience. This release of love is expressed many times in the Old Testament and the ultimate of God's love is shown in the New Testament. It is shown by God comparing His relationship to us as a marriage. We have abandoned Him. Jeremiah 2 and 3 states words of Yahweh to Jeremiah:

I remember the affection (intimacy between Israel and God within the covenant, with the accent on love) of your youth, the love of your bridal days: you followed me through the wilderness, through a lawn unsown. Israel was sacred to Yahweh, the first-fruits of his harvest; . . . shortcoming did your fathers find in me that led them to desert me? Vanity they pursued, vanity they became . . . It is long ago now since you broke your yoke, burst your bonds and said, "I will not serve" . . . "Who cares?" you said. "For I am in love with strangers and they are the ones I follow." . . . You say, "I am blameless, His anger has turned away from me." And here I am passing sentence on you because you say, "I have not sinned." If a man divorces his wife and she leaves him to marry someone else, may she still go back to him? Has not that piece of land been totally polluted? And you, who have prostituted yourself with so many lovers, you would come back to me? It is Yahweh who speaks.

. . . And you maintained a prostitute's bold front, never thinking to blush. Even then did you not cry to me, "My Father! You, the friend of my youth! Will He keep his resentment for ever, will He maintain his wrath to the end?" That was what you said, and still you went on sinning. You were so obstinate. . . . Come back, disloyal Israel... It is Yahwen who speaks. I shall frown on you no more, since I am merciful. shall not keep my resentment for ever. Only acknowledge your guilt; how you have apostatized from Yahweh your God. How you have flirted with strangers and have not listened to my voice.

These powerful chapters of Jeremiah illustrate man's relationship to his God and how we project our abandonment onto Him. In our broken relationships, we need to be aware of projecting our own guilt onto the other. We need to be able to forgive self and others. If we could unblock those negative built-up feelings, then we could possibly see what great love is awaiting us. This estrangement is felt by all at some point in life. Few see that the key is to forgive and not run away from it. Now we could start to understand with Maltz (1971) that there really is nothing to forgive because it was only a projection of our own guilt and wrong.

Leichman (1977) defined forgiveness as the process of applying goodwill to an unpleasant situation so it can be corrected. He suggested acting affirmatively, with goodwill and compassion to help dissolve the anti-human attitude and actions.

We see in these examples that forgiveness is a lovely thing, but man is more often swayed by a bitter heart and a desire for vengeance. In forgiveness, healing comes, happiness is experienced, reconciliation occurs between yourself and others, and great love can be expressed and experienced. Forgiveness can help correct the source of unpleasant situations.

12. Treatment of Forgiving

This brings us to the question, "Is failure to forgive a sin or a symptom?" (Menninger, 1974). Could an unforgiving heart be a symptom? It usually is a result of some sin that may be repressed or open that has not been dealt with, such as envy, jealousy, uncleanness, hatred, murder, drunkenness, anger, lustful pleasure (Galatians 5:19-21). Jesus had said, "The laws of Moses said, You shall not commit adultery!' But I say, Anyone who even looks at a woman with lust in his eye has already committed adultery within his heart" (Matthew 5:27-28). We do repress things or suppress them without realizing the evil that we do. The *unforgiving heart* becomes an attitude or a reaction to something within us. If we do not deal with this symptom, it tends to harden and form a crust over our lives in what the Bible would call the hardened hearts, which we discussed in an earlier section. The Pharisees had all the laws to follow, but they were unable to see their own devious ways.

The cause may be hidden from the person who has symptoms, but it still must be brought out for him to see and deal with in order to have a more vital life. As Menninger (1972) stated, symptoms can be harmful if therapists do not deal with them as the symptoms.

The inner healing ministry of Ruth Stapleton (1977) claims to deal with sin in a unique way. She tries to identify and heal repressed childhood memories. These hidden memories become rationalized and projected onto others. She states that forgiveness is the key to emotional healing.

She says we are to love our enemies. The number one enemy is oneself. Self-forgiveness is essential to self-healing.

As a man thinks in his heart, so is he. The deepest healing comes to persons who have moved beyond condemnation, beyond forgiveness, into unconditional acceptance. The hardest time to forgive is when one feels a strong reaction. One is not willing to face this reaction for what it is and within oneself will have a disturbing sense of guilt, not a willingness to forgive and accept oneself.

AA uses forgiveness in its ministry. Two of the twelve steps deal with forgiveness in their lives. First, they are to make a list of all persons they have harmed and become willing to make amends to them. They are to follow through and make direct amends to such people wherever possible, except when it might do more harm. Undergirding these forgiveness steps is the rule to put their trust and faith in a power greater than themselves and turn their lives over to God as they understand Him.

Persons grieving over the loss of a close companion often need help with forgiveness. There is a story of a woman who had back surgery. She was not recovering, and the doctors were at loose ends because they could see no reason for her relapse. They called in a minister friend and as he spoke with her, he asked if there was anything that had been bothering her. After some time she broke down and confessed that twelve years earlier she had had a terrible fight with her sister. That night her sister died suddenly, and the woman had never been able to reconcile the situation. She hadn't forgiven herself. After the confession, healing took place physically, mentally, and spiritually.

Grief studies have shown how family identification and projection in the relationship is crippling to the survivor. Many older people collapse into paralyzing illness or become withdrawn, blaming themselves for not doing the right thing before death, not making right decisions in the crisis situation, not going when called, etc. The friend, counselor, or pastor needs to help that person forgive himself and get beyond the guilt. Some of these feelings are natural but become critical when relationships are paralyzed.

We also see forgiveness coming into play when dealing with criminals. They have both guilt and anger against society. We vacillate between forgiveness, retribution, and protecting them in the society. The human being gets lost in our own collective guilt and projection. Forgiveness gets lost. If one has been punished for his crime and returned to society, many times he struggles with forgiving himself. Yet, we tend not to forgive and allow him to be free to have equal choice of work or to be as socially alive as one who has not been caught.

There is a true story of a person struggling with depression who one day became drunk, got into his car, and was caught a block from his home. The police took him to jail, stripped him nude, beat him and stripped him of all the dignity he could have. Why? The reason stated was that they were searching for drugs. What inward anger were these police releasing? Who was more wrong? Who needs to forgive?

Paul Tournier (Barclay, 1976) in *A Doctor's Case Book* quoted an instance in which a young girl had been treated for anemia without much success. As a last resort, it was decided to get her medical officer's permission to send her to a mountain sanatorium. A week later the girl brought back a report from the medical doctor at the sanatorium granting permission for her to go, even though upon analysis he did not find the same results as the other doctor. The original doctor defensively took another blood sample and found also, to his amazement, that the blood count had suddenly changed. He asked the patient if anything had happened in her life since her last visit. She replied she had suddenly been able to forgive someone against whom she had borne a nasty grudge. She now felt she could say "Yes" to life. When her mind was cured, her body also could make a change. St. Thomas Aquinas said, "Grace flows from the soul to the body."

There is a story in the Old Testament (Genesis 37:50) that is a good example of what happens in forgiveness. That is a story about Joseph, the dreamer, who interpreted Pharaoh's dream and saved Egypt from starvation. At the beginning of his adventure, there is a parallel to the parable of the forgiving servant versus the unforgiving servant.

Joseph was favored by his father, Jacob, because he was the son of Jacob's favorite wife, Rachel. When Joseph was seventeen, he came to his father and told him all the bad things his brothers were doing. He continued to grow close to his father and as a token, his father gave him a brightly colored coat. His brothers saw this favoritism and were jealous of Joseph. They raged with hatred toward him.

One night Joseph had a dream, which he proudly related, that his brothers would one day bow down to him. This really caused them to grow bitter. Then he had another dream where not only his brothers but also his father would bow down to him. Have you been in a situation like this? Joseph appears to come off self-righteous and boastful. Yet, in Jungian psychology terms, he was becoming an *individuated person*. He did not appear to have inner conflicts within himself according to his dreams. They showed a relationship with self that most of us don't reach. We can usually accept this type of person until someone else falls for their arrogance and sees them instead of us, and then our insecurities become threatened and reactions arise.

One day when Joseph's brothers did not return, Jacob sent Joseph to find them. This was their chance to kill him. Reuben, the older brother, came to his rescue. He had them put Joseph in a pit instead of killing him. He planned to come back later to get Joseph out, but some Ishmaelites came. Judah got the idea to sell Joseph for twenty shekels of silver. They then killed a goat, dipping the lovely coat in the blood to show that Joseph had died. Their father sobbed and then mourned for many weeks. He could not be comforted and the brothers' feeling of guilt caused great division in the family.

Meanwhile, in Egypt, Joseph worked for Potiphar. Potiphar's wife eyed Joseph and tried persuading him to sleep with her. Upon his refusal, she had him put in prison. Not only was Joseph sold by his brothers, but now he was wrongly tossed in prison. Was Joseph bitter? No, because God was with him, and it appeared that wherever he was, God granted him favor. The butcher and the baker of the king were tossed in prison for offending their master. They had a dream. Joseph said, "Do not the interpretations belong to God?" He interpreted the dreams, asking the butcher to remember him when he was released. Joseph again was forgotten. Later Pharaoh had two dreams that no one could interpret. Then the butcher remembered the Hebrew, Joseph. Joseph saw in Pharaoh's dream the seven good years of plenty of food and the seven lean years of famine.

Because of Joseph's insight, Pharaoh selected him to lead Egypt through this period. Joseph married Potiphar's daughter. If you recall, it was Potiphar's wife who had him tossed in prison. Joseph had two sons. The first son's name meant "God has made me forget all my hardship and all my father's house." We note here a key in living a forgiven life. He is not chained to his past experiences, filled with bitterness and resentment. The second son's name meant "For God made me fruitful in the land of my affliction." In his suffering, there was growth.

Here was a man in his thirties who had met many hardships. But what had happened in his suffering? We saw in the beginning Joseph appeared to like himself. He was on the path of *self-actualization*. He gave credit beyond himself. He later trusted God and gave God the credit for helping him through this crisis. The paradox of sin versus faith comes into play here. As an ex-prisoner, he certainly didn't have any problem getting back into society. He came out of prison to be next in line to Pharaoh. He did not project onto or blame others or God for his suffering. He didn't spend time grumbling and fighting back. He was always ready to serve and assist where he could. He was willing to risk. Paul, the Apostle, spoke of this type of living when he said to forget the past and look forward to what lies ahead.

Then the lean years came. Joseph's brothers, loaded with guilt, come back into the picture. When Joseph saw these destroyed men, he said, "You are spies." They told him about being twelve brothers but they lied about the existence of Joseph. Joseph recalled his dream. His brothers argued among themselves, haunted by the sins they had committed. They were physically drained. Joseph turned and wept. Guilt went through them because they thought God was getting even with them. They saw God as a God of vengeance. These men could not forgive themselves. They could not admit their sin. They lied to Joseph and told him their brother was dead. They thought they would never see him again and be able to reconcile the situation. This burden was a heavy one to carry around.

Joseph was thirty-nine at this time and seventeen years old when they sold him. For twenty-two years they had carried this load. They thought they now were being punished for their sin. Even though it was destroying them physically, mentally, and spiritually, they could not risk being honest even if it hurt. Man takes a risk when he confesses his sin to another, but in confession, the chains are released to a new freedom. We today carry the load around and are bound by it. We hold the guilt or wrong within. We can't forgive ourselves.

Today things are measured by time and money. Pressure of those two factors can interfere with the helping process. It is like the story of the *Little Prince* (De Saint-Exupery, 1943) when he came to earth. Whenever he asked a question, it was answered in numbers. He said:

Grown-ups love figures. When you tell them you have made a new friend, they never ask about essential matters. They never say to you, "What does his voice sound like? What games does he love best? Does he collect butterflies?" Instead, they demand: "How old is he? How many brothers has he? How much does he weigh? How much money does his father make?" Only from these figures do they think they learn anything about him. If you say to the grown-ups: "I have a beautiful house made of rosy brick, with geraniums in the window and doves on the roof," they would not be able to get any idea of the house at all. You would have to say to them, "I saw a house that cost $800,000." Then they would exclaim, "Oh, what a pretty house that is."

Back to Joseph's brothers. He gave them their grain and generously returned the money in each sack. They thought they had been set up.

In their trembling, they thought evil was being returned for evil. They saw evil in all life, a projection of their own act. They were told to bring their youngest brother, Benjamin, back with them when they returned. After receiving the money and the request for Benjamin, they were afraid to return until all their grain ran out. Their father did not trust them with Rachel's only living son, especially as they had to leave a brother behind with Joseph. Two of Jacob's sons were gone now.

After a lot of dissension, they returned with Benjamin. Joseph had a banquet for them. He had his servant wash their feet. This is similar to Jesus' Last Supper when He washed the feet of his disciples. Joseph was so touched he left the room and wept. He then asked about their father. Joseph had each of their bags filled, but in Benjamin's, he put one extra prize, his silver cup.

After a day of travel, Joseph sent his servant to bring back the one with the silver cup. They all came back upset and pleading because they had made the promise to their father to return Benjamin. Joseph, seeing their compassion and concern, revealed himself to them. He wept so loudly that his servants revealed it to Pharaoh. His brothers feared Joseph's revenge. He told them to come closer, and that God had sent him to Egypt so their lives could be preserved. He kissed each of them and told them there would be five more years of famine. He promised them the richest land in Egypt, Goshen, for their families. After returning home, they revealed to Jacob that Joseph was alive. Jacob's life was revived. He had a dream of going to Egypt and that Joseph would close his eyes in death. He risked going to the unknown land.

After Jacob's death, the brothers sent a note to Joseph saying, "Your father wants you to forgive us the evil we've done." Joseph wept. How much had he done, showing his forgiveness and love to them, and they could not see it because they had not forgiven themselves. Joseph responded, "You maybe meant evil, but God used it for good to feed people and save lives." We see that when we do not forgive ourselves, we are not open to others around us to receive their love as offered. Joseph did hit them on the head with the phrase, "You may have meant evil." There was no denying their intention or covering it up. Joseph knew what they felt. He then gives them the good news... "but God used it for good to feed people and save lives."

In the crises of life, God can use the evil brought on us for His good. This parallels the story of Christ's crucifixion. God used the evil of men for the good of us all. Yet, history shows how we in the name of Christianity persecuted the Jews. We projected our own unforgiving hearts onto them. Something happens when we accept Christ's forgiveness. There is healing in our lives. The environment becomes alive, celebrating peace and joy. On the cross, Jesus said, "Father, forgive them, for they know not what they do." That same forgiveness is present today and can be experienced for a more wholesome life. Even if we may not know what we do, He says to the Jew and all people . . . forgive, forgive, forgive!

As we see, to live in forgiveness can be a healing process for people today as well as in Biblical times. Could it be that it is a process that the medical and religious professions are taking too lightly?

13. RITUALS

One of the ways man created to deal with transitions or passages in life is rituals. A *ritual* is a solemn, repeated act, symbolizing a significant experience in the life of an individual or people. The ritual is not identical to the original action but points back to the actions.

We see with the Israelites that the Passover feast was used as a ritual. It was associated with the historical occurrence, the decisive event in the history of Israel's election, the deliverance out of Egypt. They celebrated this event to refresh the image of how God had saved His people. They were to keep this ritual as an ordinance for all times to themselves and their children. Moses said:

> When you enter the land that Yahweh is giving you, as he promised, you must keep to this ritual. And when your children ask you, "What does this ritual mean?" you will tell them, "It is the sacrifice of the Passover in honor of Yahweh who passed over the houses of the sons of Israel in Egypt, and struck Egypt but spared our houses" (Exodus 12:24-27).

Rituals are used to pass on significant events in the life of a people. Ritual is used to recall and remember this Passover event. It can be used as a promise, as the Israelites saw how God had blessed them in the past. It is also used as a means to cope with or control the pain that may be associated with passages in life. This ritual not only served as a means to recall His promises but was used as a means to equip the children for the future with knowledge of this blessing and its importance. Rituals may include for some going to a wedding, recalling that event in their own lives, sharing that event with their children, or recommitting their vows. Such events can bring joy and new life to the people.

One ritual we all have or probably will experience in our Lifetime is the funeral ceremony. The funeral is not the death, but it provides a symbolic way for people to deal with death. We read in Scripture (Genesis 23:19) that "Abraham loved Sarah, but when she died, he buried her." Here is a Biblical model for an act which of all those surrounding death is the most difficult, the one we resist most strongly (Olsson, 1979).

Burial symbolizes the isolation and the separation that death has brought. In some sense the dead person must now be put out of our life. Today many funeral directors and pastors try to ease the pain for the mourner by eliminating their presence at the graveside. We drug the one that is left behind so he or she will not have to deal with the reality directly.

The grief and loss are natural and necessary processes of life. Loss sets the stage for further creation (or more properly, recreation). When we see the rose blossom, the bud is lost; when the plant sprouts, the seed is lost. We have obvious losses in our life through the death of a loved one, breakup of an affair, separation, divorce, loss of a job, loss of money, moving, illness (loss of health), robbery, and loss of a long-term goal.

We have more subtle losses in relation to age, such as childhood dreams, puppy love, crushes, adolescent romances, leaving home, changing jobs, loss of "youth," loss of "beauty," menopause, retirement. Rituals are to be used for a person or community to help them accept or face these changes, the surrendering of our possessions, status, of whatever the loss. In thinking of bereavement, we think of those who have given "meaning, love and pain" to the dead member of the family. We think of those who have been shaped by the "meaning, love and pain" they have experienced. These rituals are also a way in which we may deal with our own dying, that final relinquishment of control. To die fully is to hand the control for yourself and your circumstances over to another and ultimately to God. This is a process of surrender that is pushed to its extreme (Olsson, 1979).

Ritual can be a means of bringing the past into the present so we may cope with the future. We use ritual to claim the power of ancient symbol and be nourished by the presence, support, and blessing of the believing community. Times are set aside for rituals. God gave the

Sabbath to man for man to use in order to rest and become strengthened in the community, worshiping and remembering all that Yahweh has done. Jesus in the Upper Room on the night prior to his crucifixion gathered his disciples together for the Last Supper (Luke 22:19-20). The Christians today celebrate the Lord's Supper in a memorial of our Lord.

We have rituals of marriage, confirmation, graduation, Easter, Christmas, Thanksgiving, etc. The celebration of the rituals for the Israelites and for us today is not to be used as an end in itself but as a means to help men reach their destiny.

The Israelites realized in the Book of Leviticus that sin, whether it be ritual uncleanness or moral fault, was a loss of vital wholeness. It is a sort of death and the remedy consists of the restoration of this wholeness. The victim, or sacrificial offering, fulfills a double role; its life symbolizes the life of the guilty one, and its death symbolizes the death that is the punishment for sin. The victim is also the intermediary by which God communicates his life to the sinner; it's the divine life. The essential point of the sacrifice was not the death of the victim, but the offering of its life. The redemptive role of the sacrifice appears in many aspects of the rituals—the Passover, in that of the daily burnt offering and daily sacrifice (Jacobs, 1958).

There is a danger in how we use rituals. The Israelites made fetishes of their rituals. They practiced the physical act but missed the real meaning. They used the time to boast of the things they had won in the past at the expense of what they could do in the future. In the writings of the prophets, we see how the Israelites turned rituals into unholy use. Many times today the church community uses rituals incorrectly. Special holidays or rituals are turned into fetishes. We see it in Corinth when Paul was speaking about their use of the Lord's Supper as an excuse to get drunk and heartlessly causing other people to go hungry (1 Corinthians 11:18-19).

We today are suffering from the lack of meaning in rituals that were to be used to pass values, tradition, or knowledge of roots on to our children in order to equip them for a more meaningful future. Meaning has been replaced by constant mobility, constant noise, constant change, constant racing for more time, constant racing for more material possession, constant need to schedule more appointments, join more clubs. We today are a nuclear family and do not share like events with many people around us. Our community is composed of divers families, and we hunger for like experience. Many feel a communal bond at Christmas. When the bond is not felt, the holidays and weekends are a time of deep depression and loneliness. We no longer know how to celebrate and find true meaning in the events of the past. Rituals that once grew out of life situations to help bring back wholeness, to reflect the past, to make the present and future more meaningful, are being lost or used as ends in themselves.

Paul (Acts 20:24-25; 36-38) experienced a farewell ritual in which many of us will take part as we move on to the next passage of life. He says:

> I reckon my own life to be worth nothing to me. I only want to complete my mission and finish the work that the Lord Jesus gave me to do. . . . And now I know none of you will ever see me again.

When Paul finished, he knelt down with them and prayed. They were all crying as they hugged and kissed him good-bye. They were especially sad because he had said that they would never see him again. And so they went with him to the ship.

As we live into Paul's rite and make it our own, we begin to experience both dying and resurrection. Effective ritual requires the loving presence of community, the quality of "witness," which is the essence of the body of Christ Paul spoke of in First Corinthians 12.

A boy named Chris (Habel, 1969, 22-24) wrote his thought on Christmas as he saw it as a joke and found God laughing. In *The Word is a Laugh*, Chris writes his experience:

> They say that Christmas is no laughing matter. But I'm not so sure about that anymore. In our house we sing Silent Night after the Christmas storm blows over. God must laugh to himself at Christmas time. Imagine 40 million toys broken in a day, 40 million fathers still assembling 40 million more, and 140 million people jamming up the stores that have the spirit of a Third World War instead of peace on earth. Just think of it, God. 40 million glasses of milk spilled on the good

tablecloth in one day, 40 million mothers with Christmas headache number 6 or 7, and just as many fathers with rather heavy hangovers from the Christmas cheer of heaven left on earth. I hope you have a sense of humor, God, as you watch our Christmas antics.

But when I think of the birth of Christ and everything that happened I know that God is smiling to himself in a very human way. Imagine 40 million angels frightening tired lazy shepherds camping out one night, or 40 dirty shepherds, smelly, hairy, bleary, scared, shivering, sleepy shepherds poking their heads through the door of a shed to look for a baby in the middle of the night. Imagine a baby bounced on a bony donkey for miles and miles, only to be born with the help of a carpenter's hands, pierced and rough and raw. Imagine a newborn baby with a red blotchy face, closed puffy eyes, screaming open mouth, healthy little bowels and call it the son of God.

Say it and smile, God. You have to! It's your son. It's your flesh! Think of it and smile! God became a human being like that. God became one of us and survived. God became like me with my pains and my pimples and my record player. Think of it and cry. The son of God is born and 40 children die because of Herod's fear. You and I are born while 40 million people die of hunger every year. Think of it and dance. For God's sense of humor is nothing else than love, a love that hurts and a love that laughs. Now God knows the joy of being human after all. God was grafted into Adam's family tree. Think of it, God, and smile. It's your Christmas tree!

14. Discipline

The Israelites were called to be a separate and obedient people. This kept them as a people with like motives, common call, laws and life-style. This did not mean that they were not to be in the community with other societies. They were called "to be a means to an end." Not only in the community were the Israelites called to be separate, but the stronger were separated from the weaker. This separation was to be used so that they could become leaders and be used to help the weaker! The separation was to be used to keep them from the influence of the "pagan" way of life, which would dilute their strengths.

Their existence was to be directed to something or someone other than themselves. Frankl (1965) has said the more one forgets oneself or gives oneself to a cause or another person, the more human he is. He said, "If I take a man as he is, I make him worse; if I take him as he ought to be, I make him become what he can be." He stated we must believe in the ideal's existence and presence and close our eyes to the fact that "humane humans" are, and probably will always remain, a minority. Each of us is challenged to join the just minority as the Israelites.

When we are not a separate people as the Israelites were called to be, we become weakened by worldly forces or community forces that leave us empty. Frankl (1967) refers to this as an *existential vacuum*. As stated previously, he saw this as a lack of traditions and values, leaving us to conform to what other people wish, reducing us to complex biochemical mechanisms. We need to unmask our hidden motives, but only to the point of confronting the genuinely human in man. This separateness is again not an excuse to be a loner or exclude and reject others.

To be a separate people, the Israelites had rigid disciplines. These disciplines were given to be used where Israel was, not where she ought to be. The disciplines set down in the Old Testament are very rigid physical realm disciplines. Christ extended the interpretation from the physical to include what one thinks or believes. Jesus extended "Thou shall not kill," saying that when one is angry at his brother, he'll answer for it in court (Matthew 5:21-22).

Webster describes *discipline* to mean training in self-control and also as training that corrects, molds, strengthens, or perfects. In psychology, we see people controlled by rigid disciplines ingrained in them by parents in ways that have been referred to as playing the tapes over and over. Again, many times in adult life, one runs away from life's disciplines and blames one's children for one's problems. Some tapes are: "Be the perfect child." "Good children don't act that way." When an adult dumps his unrealized desires on his children, he can then feel freer to go astray and sow his oats. "Don't do as I do but as I say" is the way one rationalizes irresponsibility.

These disciplines are difficult to deal with because it is so easy to project onto others rigid rules that may be inappropriate for that person or child. We struggle to accept the person where he is. We are confronted with child abuse, spouse abuse, old age abuse, abuses of all kinds. We need discipline that is a means for growth for persons individually. A community needs discipline helping us to live in love for others, seeing their needs, their hurts, and ways to strengthen each other. It should not increase others' power to destroy.

Paul warns us (Galatians 5:13) that "we are to be careful of our liberty because it will provide an opening for self-indulgence." We are to serve each other in love. If we go snapping at each other and tearing each other to pieces, we had better watch out or we will destroy the whole community.

Projection comes easy for all of us. As Freud said, we are not consciously aware of these unconscious defenses. To take the plank out of one's eye first (Matthew 7:1-5) requires discipline and a willingness to risk dropping one's conscious defenses in order to grow into wholeness with self and others.

Obedience and the laws in the Old Testament mostly dealt with man's relationship to other men. They focused on things that destroy relationships. These disciplines are not to be oppressive but used as a gift. The rules are meant to promote freedom for living in tune with all, although the Israelites abused their use and caused slavery.

In the Old Testament (Genesis 22), Abraham displayed his obedience to God. He was ready to sacrifice Isaac, his chosen son, because of a call from God. Anyone in his right mind would not sacrifice his son, anyone but Abraham and God! Abraham had to be disciplined and filled with faith and trust. One would think that probably he was quite confused. He had been told in his old age that he'd be blessed with a son and his descendants would be blessed and given this land. Now the test was put to him to kill his son as a sacrifice. As they walked to the scene, Isaac asked his father where they would get the sacrifice. Upon arrival they built the altar and arranged the wood. Isaac was bound, ready to be burnt, when Abraham heard the angelic call to stop. He had shown his fear of God and passed the test. As bystanders, we could have said this man certainly was not disciplined, but a crude, unloving parent. Psychoanalysis would have labeled Abraham paranoid. These judgments today are tough and we destroy others many times by judgment placed on them without considering the inner person! Each man has a responsibility to self and fellow man to keep both his inner and outer self under control. This mature discipline is born out of love and concern for others as well as self.

Paul (Romans 2:29) stated: "The real Jew is the one who is inwardly a Jew, and the real circumcision is in the heart—something not of the letter but of the spirit. A Jew like that may not be praised by man, but he will be praised by God."

These disciplines that control the heart are not just an outward act that others may see, but are transforming one inwardly. They may not have any outward physical evidence, but have a real meaning for one's growth in relationship to one's God and development into wholeness.

Yes, disciplines are important for our physical body, mental development and spiritual growth, so we can integrate into a whole people. Disciplines are not so rigid as to injure or kill us, but they are to be used as a means for more wholesome living.

15. Healing

Many means for healing are found in Scripture. The Psalmist sings forth much in this respect. Many people find the Psalms uplifting and healing. He points out that it is good to sing, sing praises to our Lord (Psalms 147). The Psalmist says Yahweh will heal the broken-hearted and bind up their wounds. In pure praise there is no element of self, but there is only simple adoration, which brings us in tune with God. In 1 Samuel 16:14-23 Saul was troubled with an evil spirit from God when David took the harp and played. Saul grew calm and recovered as the evil spirit left him. The calming of music can bring healing.

Paul found rejoicing in his suffering (Colossians 1:24) as healing. He found meaning or a purpose in his suffering by getting beyond himself. Neal (1972) encourages us to offer our pain as a sacrifice for someone else's healing. As a result, healing comes to us. Paul experienced this dynamic in his suffering.

Paul gives us another alternative in Ephesians 5:20, to give thanks in all circumstances. This is a choice to find thanks and something to be thankful for in whatever circumstance we're in. Thanksgiving is being thankful for life because we as humans can not always differentiate the good from the bad. Our struggle may be a blessing in disguise.

This past spring a neighbor boy of seventeen died of a stroke suddenly. He was an only son among seven children. His mother, who has multiple sclerosis and is crippled to the point of needing a wheelchair, offered thanksgiving through her tears while grieving the loss of her son. She said, "I can only thank God for the beautiful seventeen years I had with my son." Healing came to her and others in the funeral home through her expression of thanksgiving

In Jesus' healing ministry, he continually proclaimed, "Thy faith has made thee whole" (Matthew 9:22). There is a trust in the Power beyond ourselves, a trust in the Lord that brings about a healing that none of us can really explain, but yet we see and hear of its miraculous power today.

Jesus withdrew and found healing in prayer, a solitude with God. We also have that opportunity to withdraw, spending time in meditation, being in solitude alone, and having peace of mind and a new healing strength come to us. Much is being discovered today through meditation, the study of the different Eastern religions, and their practice of meditation and healing through this discipline. "Be still and know I am God" (Psalms 46:10). A gal shared with me her experience of divorce and the suffering and anguish she knew. She finally got through the crisis when she was told the Psalmist's message to "Be still." She tried it, quitting the fighting and searching everywhere for an answer.

Throughout Scripture, we are reminded to confess our Sins and that then a cleansing and new freedom comes Matthew 3:6). Confession in Scripture symbolized purification. We see this in Leviticus, with the different cleansing and purification rites. In each of the different ways mentioned above an offering takes place, an offering of thanksgiving, an offering of our suffering for another, an offering of our sacrifice, an offering of our joy, and an offering of ourselves. In making an offering, it is very important what we offer and how. The attitude in which the offering is given seems to be a key—offering with joy, with thanksgiving, and with praise. This offering may have to do with our thoughts—"For as he thinketh in his heart, so is he" (Proverbs 23:7).

We are to be patient and allow the healing process to have an appropriate climate conductive to healing. "Wait upon the Lord."

Healing comes through self-surrender. We see in Jesus' ministry people coming to him, surrendering themselves into the hands of their Lord. Paul surrendered as he stated, "Not I, but Christ, liveth in me" (Galatians 2:20). This again requires letting down our ego defenses and letting go so we can get beyond ourselves.

Healing comes when we hear and obey, "Be not anxious about tomorrow," and also do not let fears and frustrations overpower us. As Peter was walking on water, he took his eyes off of Jesus, fear overcame him, and he went down (Matthew 14:30). When obstacles and not God become our reality, then we also sink and drown.

Ministering to the healing of others can be a costly sacrifice if we really want to be serious about the mission or the call to heal. The reward is there if the heart is willing. Jung (1933) says:

> The truly religious person has a attitude or human quality that has a kind of deep respect for facts and wants, and also for the person who suffers from them—a respect for the secret of such a human life. He knows God had brought all sorts of strange and inconceivable things to pass, and seeks in the most curious ways to enter a man's heart. He senses in everything the unseen presence of the Divine Will. He has an "unprejudiced objective." We cannot change anything unless we accept it. Condemnation does not liberate, it oppresses. If a doctor wishes to help a human being he must be able to accept him. He can do this only when he has already seen and accepted himself as he is.

This thought brings forth again Jesus' warning for us, "Judge not, or ye shall be judged." When we condemn, as Jung says, we do not liberate but oppress. We may then be projecting some of our own weaknesses on the human being who seeks to get free from the claims that oppress him.

Jung (1933) says that the larger number of psychotherapists are disciples of Freud and Adler. This means that the greater number of patients are alienated from a spiritual standpoint. He also says he saw that patients over thirty-five found their problems, when they really get down to it, were their religious perspective on life.

There is meaning in life and there is a side of each of us that seeks and searches to become awake and aware of our inner call to find that "pearl of great price" (Matthew 13:45-46). We have seen here how people of God have struggled throughout history to find meaning in life. They find it in their God directing and giving meaning and healing to life even though man inevitably deserts His way and strays into the wilderness.

References

Clown Ministry Workshop. Washington, D.C., February-June 1979

Norem, Bonnie. "Forgiveness Talk," Fairfax, Va., February 1977.

———. "Paralytic Talk," Fairfax, Va., February 1975.

O'Conner, Elizabeth. "Exodus Talk," Washington, D.C., March 1979

———. "Unity Talk," Washington, D.C., July 1979.

Sanford, John. Seminar: Jonah in the Whale, Washington, D.C.
    February 1979.

———. Seminar: Journey into Wholeness, St. Simon's Island, May 1978.

Thomas, J. Bi/Polar Teacher's Seminar, Dallas, April 1979.

Bibliography

Reference List

Barclay, William. *And He Had Compassion*. Valley Forge: Judson Press, 1976.

——. *And Jesus Said*. Philadelphia: Westminister Press, 1976.

——.*Gospel of John, Volume I*. Philadelphia: Westminister Press, 1975

Boelter, Francis W. *The Covenant People of God*. Nashville: Tidings, 1971.

Bonhoeffer, Dietrich. *Life Together*. New York: Harper & Row, 1954.

Cobb, John. *To Pray or Not to Pray*. Nashville: Upper Room, 1974.

De Castillijo, Irene Clarement. *Knowing Women*. New York: Harper Colophon Books, 1973.

De Saint-Exupery, Antoine. *The Little Prince*. New York: Harcourt, Втасе, 1943.

Drescher, John. *If I Were Starting My Family Again*. Nashville: Abingdon Press, 1979.

Edwards, Tilden. *Living Simply through the Day*. New York: Paulist Press, 1977.

Erikson, Eric. *Childhood & Society*. New York: Norton, 1964.

Frankl, Viktor. *The Doctor and the Soul*. New York: Alfred A. Knopf, 1965.

——. *Man's Search for Meaning*. New York: Norton, 1967.

——. *Unconscious God*. New York: Simon & Schuster, 1975.

Fromm, Erich. *The Heart of Man*. New York: Harper & Row, 1968.

Habel, Norman C. *For Mature Adults Only*. Philadelphia: Fortress Press, 1969.

Jacobs, Edmond. *Theology of the Old Testament*. New York: Harper & Row, 1958.

Jerusalem Bible.

Jones, R, and J. Horn. "The Third Wave: Nazism in High School," *Psychology Today*, July 1976, pp.14-16.

Jung, Carl G. *Modern Man in Search of a Soul*. New York: Harcourt,

Brace & World, 1933.

Kierkegaard, S. Sickness unto Death. Garden City: Doubleday & Co. 1954

Leichtman, Robert and Carl Japike. *Cultivating Tolerance and Forgiveness.* Columbus: Ariel Press, 1977.

Maltz, Maxwell. *Psycho-Cybernetics.* New Holland: Wilshire, 1971.

May, Rollo. *Love and Will.* New York: W. W. Norton, 1969.

———. *Man's Search for Himself.* New York: Harcourt, Brace and World, 1933.

Menninger, Karl. *The Crime of Punishment.* New York: Viking Press, 1968.

———. *Whatever Became of Sin?* New York: Hawthorne Books, 1974.

Neal, Emily Gardiner. *The Healing Power of Christ.* New York: Hawthorne, 1972.

Nouwen, Henri J. W. *Clowning in Rome.* Garden City: Image Books, 1979.

Olsson, Karl A. *When the Road Bends.* Minneapolis: Augsburg Publishing House, 1979.

Parker, Colin Murray. Bereavement: *Studies of Grief in Adult Life.* International University Press, 1972.

Rowly, Peter. *New Gods in America.* New York: McKay Co., 1971.

Sanford, John A. *Healing and Wholeness.* New York: Paulist Press, 1977

———. *The Kingdom Within*, Philadelphia: J. B. Lippincott, 1970.

Schlink, Basilen. *You Will Never Be the Same.* London: Bethany Fellowship, 1972.

Sheehy, Gail. *Passages.* New York: E.P. Dutton, 1974.

Skoyland, Elizabeth R. *The Whole Christian.* New York: Harper & Row, 1976.

Stapleton, Ruth Carter *The Gift of Inner Healing.* Waco: Word, 1977.

Ten Boom, Corrie. *Tramp for the Lord.* Old Tappan: Fleming H. Revell, Co., 1974.

Thomas, J. W. *Bi/Polar: A Positive Way of Understanding People.* Dallas: Tayton Publishing Co., 1978.

Two Listeners. *God Calling.* Old Tappan: Spire Books, 1977.

www.ingramcontent.com/pod-product-compliance
Lightning Source LLC
Chambersburg PA
CBHW051232120626
46547CB00013B/1612